ISBN 978-1-331-78097-7
PIBN 10233844

This book is a reproduction of an important historical work. Forgotten Books uses state-of-the-art technology to digitally reconstruct the work, preserving the original format whilst repairing imperfections present in the aged copy. In rare cases, an imperfection in the original, such as a blemish or missing page, may be replicated in our edition. We do, however, repair the vast majority of imperfections successfully; any imperfections that remain are intentionally left to preserve the state of such historical works.

English
Français
Deutsche
Italiano
Español
Português

www.forgottenbooks.com

Mythology Photography **Fiction**
Fishing Christianity **Art** Cooking
Essays Buddhism Freemasonry
Medicine **Biology** Music **Ancient**
Egypt Evolution Carpentry Physics
Dance Geology **Mathematics** Fitness
Shakespeare **Folklore** Yoga Marketing
Confidence Immortality Biographies
Poetry **Psychology** Witchcraft
Electronics Chemistry History **Law**
Accounting **Philosophy** Anthropology
Alchemy Drama Quantum Mechanics
Atheism Sexual Health **Ancient History**
Entrepreneurship Languages Sport
Paleontology Needlework Islam
Metaphysics Investment Archaeology
Parenting Statistics Criminology
Motivational

CONTENTS

"HORAS NON NUMERO NISI SERENAS"

TO MY SUNDIAL

" I count the bright hours only "—that is well :
 From cloud and shadow to avert the eye,
 To sunny moments only, as they fly,
Thy gaze to give, and all their story tell.

And yet, methinks, thou losest much the while,
 For eyes part-closéd see not all the truth,
 Whether the thing shut out be joy or ruth ;
Clear suns make happy, but they may beguile.

Scan thou the roses that around thee cling,
 Do not their colours purer, richer, show,
 In light subdued, than in the glaring glow
Of noontide suns, that no soft shading bring ?

And when the rain, or midnight dews, that fall
 From unsunned heavens, their petals wet,
 Does not their fragrance, with the mignonette,
Far sweeter rise, the senses to enthrall ?

A

While all earth's toilers, man and beast alike,
   Their tasks less irksome find, of brain, hands,
      feet,
   In clouded hours, than in the withering heat
Of brazen skies whose beams oft cruel strike !

And so, 'tis only partly I agree,
   Gay friend, to let but bright hours find a place
   On memory's tablets, and all else efface
That would, remembered, black and gloomy be.

I own, with thee, prosperity is good,
   Much to be sought ; much prized as Heaven's
      gift ;
   While to adversity I'd give short shrift,
Which, by itself, but feeds the morbid mood.

With thee, all shadows of the past I'd ban
   From memory, if they do but dim the eyes
   With tears, and all fresh effort paralyse ;
Such *utter* gloom let all forget who can !

Yes, " count the sunny hours," sing I with thee,
   The hours when light, love, gladness, have
      inspired
   Our drooping hearts ; when hope, new-born,
      hath fired
Our laggard lives to new activity.

But, 'mong these, mark those frequent precious
    hours,
  When, spite of shower and shadow, roses rare
  Of joy and comfort, blossomed to the air,
And heavenly peace, like perfume, filled the
    bowers.

Omit not from the sum, good friend, I pray,
  The seasons oft, when, clear ev'n in the cloud,
  The bright light shone, and called forth praises
    loud,
Through all the dreary, darksome, dragging day.

Nor e'er forget those moments of surprise,
  When, passing gloomy vales of weeping through,
  Clear wells of sweet refreshing sprang to view,
That lit with wonder the adoring eyes.

Write these, I ask, in number manifold,
  Among the hours of glory thou dost count—
  To what proportions will the total mount !
Nor will their shining tale be ever told !

Then, too, I vow, thy motto shall be mine !
  And we shall not be idle, thou and I ;
  For bright hours cease not, to the seeing eye,
And will outrun the dark, while Love doth shine !

A TASTE OF LIFE

I TASTED glorious life to-day,
  My cup was running o'er ;
With joy of June my cup was full,
  I had no room for more.

The blazing blooms around the lake,
  Beneath the azure sky,
Were mirrored in its ruddy face,
  That shimmered dreamily.

The hum of myriad insect wings
  Was music in my ear,
And mystic choirs invisible
  Attuned their anthems near.

The fragrance of a thousand flowers,
  Athwart the shining lea,
Was borne upon the gentle breeze
  To swell my ecstasy.

Through every portal of my soul
  High noon its glories poured,
And flooded out with loveliness
  Each shadow of discord,

Till one great glowing rapture held
 My spirit in its power,
And past and future met and merged
 In that consummate hour.

And had its golden moments turned
 Into eternity,
Its pure, transporting, crowded bliss
 Were Heaven's gate to me !

SONG

As rivers to the ocean,
   As swallows to the blue,
As roses to the sunlight,
   So turn my thoughts to you.

The rivers seek the ocean,
   Their turmoil to allay ;
So end my weary frettings
   When forth to you I stray.

The swallows love the breezes
   That brace them in the blue ;
So mount my thoughts and fancies
   To purer heights in you.

The roses greet the sunlight
   That makes them live and glow ;
And in your radiance only
   Can I true pleasure know.

As rivers to the ocean,
   As swallows to the blue,
As roses to the sunlight,
   So turn my thoughts to you.

SURVIVAL

TO A FAVOURITE TREE BLOWN DOWN BY THE STORM

FRIEND ! must I mourn thee dead, as here I see
    thee lie,
Laid low the honoured head, that tapered to the
    sky ?

Ah, gone, for ever gone, thy loveliness and charm
Of summer green, that won my admiration warm !

Sweet shelter nevermore thy branches wide shall
    yield,
From sun, or storms that roar across the open field !

Nor ever shall I hear again the burst of song,
From birds that carolled clear, thy fragrant boughs
    among !

And yet, methinks 'twere wrong to call thee wholly
    dead,
Though beauty, shelter, song, with thee have
    perishéd !

Sure something shall survive, of that which thou
    hast been,
To show thee still alive, though changed the form
    and scene !

When o'er the wintry hearth the Yule-log blazes
  bright,
Amid the jocund mirth, we'll thank *thee* for its light !

When over dyke and stream I rear bridge, step, or
  stile,
In ev'ry plank and beam I'll praise *thy* help the
  while !

And when, from spoilers' raid, my nursling trees
  demand
Stout fences, fitly made *thy* timbers I'll command !

And so, though thy dear face I ne'er again shall see,
In what's bequeathed I'll trace thy former energy !

If beauty, shelter, song, erst thine, transmuted be
To light, help, safety, long shall live thy memory !

And mortals all may learn a lesson even from thee,
How likewise they may earn sure immortality !

For if, from thoughts, words, deeds, some small
  converted part
Of after worth proceeds, to cheer some future heart ;

Then, though our days be told, and though departed
  we,
Posterity shall hold a cherished legacy !

THE SNOWDROP

TO A CHILD

I WENT into the garden,
  To see what I could find,
And there I saw a snowdrop,
  A-nodding in the wind.

I said, " Good-day, dear snowdrop,
  I'm glad to see you here."
It said, " I've come to tell you
  The merry Spring is near."

I said, " Sweet snowdrop, tell me
  Where have you been so long ? "
It said, " Oh, that's a secret,
  To tell you would be wrong."

I said, " But were you dead, dear ? "
  It said, " Oh, not at all,
I went away, because, Sir,
  I heard the fairies call,—

I needed a new helmet,
  The old was nearly done ;
They gave me this snow-white one,
  To glitter in the sun,—

My spear was worn and bent, too,
   Not fit, Sir, to be seen ;
The fairies made this new one,
   So straight, and tall, and green."

I said, " Sweet darling snowdrop,
   Pray tell me, tell me true,
Will fairies in the far land
   Give *me* new armour too ? "

" Oh yes," it said—and seven times
   It nodded in the breeze ;
And so I said, " I thank you,
   Your answer well doth please,—

You're kind," I said, " to bring me
   Glad tidings of the Spring,
To tell me, too, of gardens
   Where fairies dance and sing,—

And so I'll come, dear snowdrop,
   To see you ev'ry day,
To coax you by my kindness
   To make a long, long stay."

The snowdrop made a curtsy,
   And when I turned to go,
The world was full of sunshine,
   My heart was all a-glow.

LOST MUSIC

To-DAY I saw a sorry sight,
Two birds of song in mortal fight :
So eager in the senseless fray,
They never saw me in the way,—
    Though deemed their common enemy !
Ashamed, I thought to end them both,
But rising pity made me loth
    To make them pay the penalty.

No wonder I had missed their song,
The tall trees' topmost boughs among !
No wonder I looked up in vain,
To catch their old familiar strain
    Of pure, inspiring melody,
When beak, and claw, and soaring wing,
Low-aimed, were spent fierce feud to fling,
    In bitter, stupid rivalry !

To-day we see a sorry sight,
When wrangling Churches jealous fight :
Not striving which shall loudest sing
The tidings that alone can bring
    To nought, the common enemy ;
But wasting hand, and heart, and brain,
In wicked warfare, to obtain
    Some selfish, worldly victory.

IN MEMORIAM: T. K.

"*Nympha pudica Deum vidit, et erubuit*"

"THE modest Water saw her God, and blushed"—
'Twas thus, friend, Crashaw's epigram we read
Together here; nor dreamed that, ere had sped
One moon, the one or other should lie hushed
In death; that Heaven's best wine, like that which
    gushed
From Cana's vessels, radiant and red,
At bidding of the Master, in the stead
Of water, should be thine; and fond hearts, crushed
With sorrow, left behind! O mystery!
Thine now, pure soul, that " vision of the God "
The Water saw! Thine, too, the ecstasy
And " blush " on brow, of those in Heaven's abode
Who, " modest," hear the Bridegroom's voice, and
    see
His face of glory,—then, lay down each load!

WILD HYACINTHS

When Hyacinthus' life-blood stained the ground,
(The Darling of Apollo), from the blow
Of spiteful Zephyrus (ah, day of woe !)
Then, at great Phœbus' edict, 'mid the sound
Of mighty weeping, your fresh blooms were found,
The purple offspring !   So, the world doth know
For ever, the god's anguish !   And ye throw
Your sweet memorial clusters all around !

How strange and true !   That fairest flowers have
    sprung
Where love has bled !   That, watered by salt tears,
Rare golden fruits on trees of ruth have hung !
That red joy-blossoms oft crown prickly fears !
So, all this beauty I see broadcast flung,
In purpling woodlands, the lost god endears !

NEVERMORE

THE hearts of children answer true
To all the notes of mirth and rue,
But one thing strikes me o'er and o'er,
They have no ear for " Nevermore ! "

Their life one rosy Present is :
What lies behind they scarcely miss ;
All boundless is their view before,
Yet ne'er a dream of " Nevermore " !

They lightly prate of pleasures gone,
Rare days of frolic, feast, and fun :
Oh, happy blindness ! They ignore
That each is labelled " Nevermore " !

Big burning tears of grief they shed,
When told of dear friends vanishéd ;
But taste not sorrow's deepest core,—
The bitterness of " Nevermore " 1

'Tis wisely, kindly, ordered so :
For why, too soon, should young hearts know
The tragedy and anguish sore,
Struck with the weird note " Nevermore " !

CROCUSES

WHEN I behold you hail the Sun to-day,
With open petals laughing to the blue ;
Methinks the old Greek mythic story true,
That, where Zeus, Father of the gods, once lay,
With giant limbs outstretched, one amorous day,
You sprang ; his hot blood kindling fires, which you
From burning ground did fling in flames, whose hue
Of gold, doth still, each Spring, his haunts betray !

And so, the sweet thrill from these primal heats
   Of the young year, to your quick sense recalls
That visit of the god !   My heart, too, beats,
   Like yours, responsive !   His warm touch en-
      thralls !
Oh ! would 'twere known, that Heav'n in like wise
      greets
   The world of men,—and to like glory calls !

THE NEARER LOOK

WHO thinks to look at the Sun,
  But strikes himself blind !
His zeal doth his wisdom outrun,
  And leave it behind !
Let him look at the earth, with its wonderful store
Of light and of colour, of beauty galore ;
Its blossom and fruit, its pure joys evermore,—
  And what's hid in the Sun he will find !

Who thinks to look upon God,
  For nought his strength spends ;
To search for Him, after such mode,
  In vanity ends !
Let him look where, resplendent, in lives all around,
Truth, purity, love, deeds unselfish abound,—
Which never in Nature's own garden were found,—
  And what God is, he soon apprehends !

16

STRUGGLE

WITHOUT, as I heard the wild winds roar,
And saw the black clouds their floods outpour,
    As the lightnings flashed,
    And the thunders crashed,
And the hurricane's force waxed more and more,
    I said, as I looked from my window warm,
    " Heav'n never on me send such a storm ! "

Then came a dark day, when fierce and fast,
Down fell on my head the blinding blast !
    Yet tho' sore assailed,
    I nor shrank nor quailed,
For tho' loud the gale raged, as 'twould rage its last,
    The struggle I waged, as I journeyed on,
    Awoke in me powers before unknown !

I felt my hot blood a-tingling flow ;
With thrill of the fight my soul did glow ;
    And when, braced and pure,
    I emerged secure
From the strife that had tried my courage so,
    I said, " Let Heav'n send me or sun or rain,
    I'll never know flinching fear again ! "

LOVE, THE LEVER

THEY thought to heal me, when they cast
  Reproving glances towards me ;
As if their proud contempt could shrive me
Of my sin, or scorn could drive me
  E'er to mend my ways,—
  Liefer end my days !

They thought to lift me, when they held
  A pattern pure above me ;
As if to gaze on cold perfection
Ever could give new direction
  To my wrecked desires ;
  Or awake new fires !

Then came a voice of cadence sweet,
  And winning tones that touched me,
" I love thee, friend "—and, deeply welling
In my soul, and all-compelling,
  Love leapt at the sound ;
  Life and Heaven I found !

SONG

Come to me with the Spring,
  With the dazzling daffodil ;
When the buds that ope on every spray,
And the song that bursts at break of day
  My thoughts with thine image fill,—
  Come with the daffodil !

Come when the Summer's high,
  With the lily and the rose ;
When the world is all a garden fair,
And a thousand floating perfumes rare
  Wake all a poor lover's woes,—
  Come with lily and rose !

Come with the Autumn dews,
  With the golden harvest-tide ;
When the smiling fields are decked with sheaves,
And the Earth her robes of russet weaves,
  And red is the mountain side,—
  Come with the harvest-tide !

Come with the Winter wild,
  With the bitter frost and snow ;

When enwrapped in death-sleep all things seem,
And through all the darksome days I dream
   Of love that no death can know,—
   Come,—nor again, Love, go !

GAIN IN LOSS

If no cloudlets fringe the East,
  Ere the sun mounts up the skies,
Then, no glorious colour-feast
    To the eyes !

If no whirling, stormy breeze
  Stir the air's unruffled calm,
Then, no music in the trees
    With its balm !

If no dripping rain descends,
  In the golden summertide,
Then, no scent the brier sends,
    Far and wide !

So, when cloud, or storm, or rain,
  Would oppress my spirit sore,
I still say " There's some great gain
    At the core ! "

DAFFODILS

IN A SHOP WINDOW

Love you I must, ye fair, sweet daffodils,
Though born of heats before wild Nature wills !
Your glowing yellow heads, and tall green spears,
Your old-world spell, your memories of past years,
Your open throats that trumpet forth the Spring,
Your thousand glamours—all, I needs must sing !
Yet liefer had I seen you in the field
Full two months hence, where Mother Earth doth
    yield,
In her own proper season, herb and flower ;
Nor borrows other aids than sun and shower !
Not wise, methinks, to force high Heaven's hand,
To choose to come or go, to fall or stand ;
If forced the bloom, the sooner comes decay,—
Give Time her leisure, and give Hope her day,
'Tis best to live and die as Nature wills,
Best both for mortal men, and daffodils.

NEW YEAR'S EVE

THE Old Year hastens to its close,
And hark ! how drear the tempest blows !
A few dark hours, and all is o'er,
The dying year will be no more !

Ah then, asleep with other years,
And buried all its smiles and tears,
Gone and forgotten let it lie,
Its tale will follow by and by !

Be grateful for the joy it brought,
Be sure its pain was not for nought ;
Its discipline was all for gain,
Not one of all its smarts in vain !

And so, as strikes the midnight bell,
Smile in the New Year ; wish it well ;
If thou still patient be, and true,
'Twill then both " Happy " be, and " New " !

VISION

A FRAGMENT

ALL is pure, to the eye that's pure ;
    All, to the heart that knows, is wise ;
Truth, to the true, abides most sure,
    Love, to the loving, never dies.

NEW YEAR'S MORN

'Tis gone !   And though I hear a sigh,
The tall trees through, that years should die ;
Though breathless else all Nature lies,
And stillness rules the silent skies,
No grief for dead years here I see,
But pent-up, hushed expectancy !

For on yon East horizon clear,
Bright Hope, newborn, sees promise near
Of Good, which, from the days of yore,
Men's dreams have visioned on before ;
And now, on tip-toe all things stand,
To sight the consummation grand !

THE STORM-FIEND

In the gathering night I stood,
  On the edge of the sheltering wood,
And, as swift o'er the heavens the dark clouds sped
Where I looked for the wild-fowl to come overhead
  To the gun I held in hand,
  On the watch I still kept stand.

On the left, where the clouds were riven,
  I espied a great heron, driven
By the gale, sweep to earth, where a tumbling
    brook
Offered prey, but its flight of a sudden it took,
  At the scent of danger near,
  On its ghostly wings of fear.

Then, as louder arose the howl
  Of the blast, as I listened, an owl
Hooted high its complaint to the angry winds ;
And a bird, with the swoop of a hawk, when it finds
  Its poor victim, dropped and rose—
  And still the night wilder grows !

Queer companions, and weird, methought !
  Even a wandering lapwing sought,

26

With a wail of alarm, to chide the storm,
For whirling her out of a corner warm,
    Where, forlorn and tempest-stayed,
    She her lonely bed had made.

So, as never a duck did fly
To my gun, in the lowering sky,
With a look to the East, where, dark and bold,
O'er the serried tree-tops tall and old,
    Loomed the lofty towers of home,
    My eyes still beyond did roam.

For, away on the farthest brink
Of the heavens now black as ink,
There opened a blue bewitching eye,
And there, in its centre, with mischief sly,
    There twinkled a silver star,
    That jeered at me from afar.

And then I perceived at a glance,
That the storm-fiend had led me a dance,
And I said, as I groped my homeward path,
With feelings that swung betwixt mirth and wrath,
    " I will not attempt to deny
    'Twas the storm had the sport, not I."

CHRISTMAS CAROL

Down to our world, so drear and old,
  In the dim long ago,
Forth from Thy Father's joys untold,
  Saviour-Child, Thou didst go.
Angels Thy glorious coming sang,
  While the stars gazed below ;
O'er the glad earth the tidings rang,
  In the dim long ago.

For the world's gloom, and care, and sin,
  In the dim long ago,
Light and salvation Thou didst win,
  Balm for its pain and woe.
Sorrow to singing quick did turn,
  Thou didst but speak, and lo,
Hearts that were dead, with love did burn,
  In the dim long ago.

Into my world, Lord Jesus, come,
  Now, as in long ago,
Make this poor heart, so cold and dumb,
  Rich with Thy goodness grow.

And when in darkness, Saviour dear,
  Sadness and fear I know,
Let me the song of angels hear,
  Now, as in long ago.

Into Thy Church, grown faint and lone,
  As in the long ago,
Come with new might and mercy down,
  Make its dull heart to glow.
And by Thy Word made pure and strong,
  Conquering ev'ry foe,
Let its full voice break forth with song,
  As in the long ago.

THE LINKED AGES

AT KAIMS CASTLE

CHILDREN playing where the Roman lay !
Oh what a change from that far-off day,
When Agricola's legions, o'erwhelming the land,
Here, on this high green mound, made stand,
Threw up this trench, and in grim dark rage,
Waited fierce Galgacus' hordes to engage !

Brave, blind heroes !   Yet surely led here,
Unknowing, to bring the blest knowledge more near,
Of Heaven's truth to our land.   So these children
    to-day
Shout and dance, laugh and sing, in the sunshine
    gay,
Nor think that the gladness which makes their
    hearts glow,
Was so painfully won in the stern long ago.

Ah, 'tis ever the same as the years roll on ;
We forget what we owe to the great ones gone,—
That our freedom and peace, and each day's new
    joys
Have been won 'mid the clash and the harsh, rude
    noise

30

Of conflict and struggle, oft blind, but sincere,
Which Love turned to good in the distant year.

And so will it be in the far coming days ;
Our children's children will sing in the ways,
Only if we, like the warriors of old,
Fight for the best, by the truth made bold ;
Then will our sons, like these children to-day,
Dance on our deeds, when we've long passed away.

THE KEY OF THE FUTURE

(JOSHUA V. 13-15)

THE chequered past lay all behind, a many-coloured
    field,
Its triumphs, failures, doubts and fears, for ever.
    closed and sealed,
And on the threshold of the future, new and all
    unknown,
Brave Joshua faced the opposing darkness, pensive
    and alone.

From out the gloom a figure grim loomed threaten-
    ing in the path,
A warrior stern, with sword unsheathed, all
    panoplied in wrath,
" For us or for our adversaries ? " prompt our
    hero cried,
Demanding if as foe he came, or on Jehovah's side.

But not a word the Stranger spake, the mystery to
    unveil !
Not Joshua's was it then to know of future things
    the tale,

32

The present only was his care, and that was " holy
    ground,"
In reverent service day by day would victory be
    found.

Thus, oft upon the verge of years, departed and to
    come,
This sudden apparition will with terror strike us
    dumb,—
Some giant evil in the way, in gleaming armour
    dread,
That seems to mark the bound betwixt the living
    and the dead.

But, spite of all our fierce demands his errands dark
    to know,
Our challenger will still refuse to answer " Friend
    or foe " ;
Not ours to know the end of all the mystic coming
    days,
Or whether seeming perils shall yet call for loudest
    praise.

The key of all the future, whether ominous or bright,
Is in the present hour—in constant reverence for the
    right ;
" What saith the Lord unto His servant ? " thence
    doth duty spring,
Thence safety, peace, and triumph rise, whate'er the
    years may bring.

KIND CRUELTY

TO THE MOON

FAIR Goddess !   Sung by many tongues of old,
   To-night a golden crescent in the blue,
   Hung out as if to claim the reverent view,
Dip not behind yon hill till thou have told
If other eyes I know thy face behold—
   Eyes like the azure which encircles thee !
   Oh ! but to know that she, too, turns to thee
With thoughts akin to those which now I hold—
Sweet thoughts of love—love that makes all things
     glow,
   That knitteth Heaven and this fair earth in one.
Tell me before thine edge be sunk too low
   If she—ah, cruel moon : and art thou gone ?
Denying me her present mind to know,
   Or if with mine her heart's in unison !

(A YEAR AFTER)

Methinks, fair orb, thou seemest half ashamed ;
   Thy harvest-crimson blush betrayeth thee,
   And thou dost hide thy face so timidly
Behind yon cloud, as if thy fault I blamed,

34

When thou withheld'st the fond reply I claimed.
  Nay, fear not, shrinking moon, for thou didst well
  To hide the truth, and let her own lips tell !
Yes ! She herself hath now the answer framed,
Which thou so wisely didst forbear to say ;
  In tokens thou couldst not command it fell—
Her drooping eye, wherein love struggling lay,
  Her blush, her happy tears, combined to spell
That word thou didst, in goodness, not betray,
  So, thy kind cruelty did serve me well.

SPRING SONG

It's on the wing, it's on the way,
  I saw it laugh this morning;
It dances nearer every day,
  The lingering darkness scorning,—
    Come, Spring, I'll sing thee,
    In lightsome measure sing thee,
    With blithesome pleasure sing thee,
    O come, Spring, come.

It's on the wing, it's on the way,
  It peeped in at my window;
I would not give its gleeful ray,
  For all the wealth of Ind, O,—
    Come, Spring, I'll sing thee,
    Etc., etc., etc.

It's on the wing, it's on the way,
  The smiling snowdrop tells me
Cold winter soon must haste away,
  And mirth to song compels me,—
    Come, Spring, I'll sing thee,
    Etc., etc., etc.

It's on the wing, it's on the way,
  The throstle gaily greets it,

Salutes it with a roundelay,
  And loud and long repeats it,—
    ` Come, Spring, I'll sing thee,
        Etc., etc., etc.

It's on the wing, it's on the way,
  It's breath already warms me
With promises of blossoms gay,
  And music sweet that charms me,—
    Come, Spring, I'll sing thee,
    In lightsome measure sing thee,
    With blithesome pleasure sing thee,
      O come, Spring, come.

A WINTER SKY-SCAPE

COMET 1910 A

BEHIND, the gleaming silver moon in wintry sky of
    blue ;
Before, on white snow-mantled ground, my figure
    shadowed true ;
And o'er the scene, with shadows weird from dark-
    ling tower and tree,
A solemn hush, the spell of night, a pale cold mystery.

Away to westward 'gainst the sky, as keeping
    watch the while,
Tall firs like sentinels lift their heads in bold
    unbroken file ;
And through and 'yond them, glowing still, where
    late the sun has died,
From daffodil to crimson blush the lingering
    eventide.

A fairy scene, those mingling hues ! To Fancy's
    eye transformed
To seas of gold and yellow sands, by constant
    summers warmed ;

28

And see ! a thousand creeks and bays the broken
    cloudland shows,
With shining reefs and islets fair, begirt with shores
    of rose.

But look, where pales to faintest blue the many-
    coloured sky,
What mystic shape of light appears, to hold the
    ravished eye ?
A dazzling ball of fire, descending swift to catch the
    sun,
With trailing splendour upwards cast, of beams
    celestial spun !

O miracle of force and flame, a thousand eyes this
    hour,
A thousand minds, the wide world o'er, are strain-
    ing every power
The wonders of thy form and substance fully to
    unfold,
Through what untravelled spaces thou hast come,
    what spheres untold !

And millions in benighted lands look up in dread
    and fear,—
An awful omen thou, to them, of plague and horror
    near !
To revolution, blood, and fire, to rapine and red
    war,
They hear thy dire disastrous summons, sounding
    from afar !

All this to them—but as again I scan my fairy
  scene,
Thou art a part of what I see ; and in that bay
  serene
Where floating cloudlets hem thee in, to me thou
  dost appear
A phantom ship on smiling seas, sailing in full
  career.

Thy hull of flame is ploughing fast those wavelets
  of my dream,
Thy great white sails, with list to port, in towering
  glory gleam ;
All nature, bent and breathless, waits to see thy
  voyage done,
And lo ! even as I look, thou hast at last the haven
  won !

In such a hush, on such a sea, at such an eventide,
Heaven send its shining bark to bear me to the
  other side ;
Through glowing seas with golden shores my voyage
  be as this,
Till in far harbours, safe and calm, I reach the land
  of bliss.

EVENSONG

THE birds sing out in the morning
    Their loud and lusty lay,
Sing merrily out in the morning,
    When breaks the golden day.

Anon, in the dazzling noontide,
    As rolls the day along,
In the dazzling, dusty noontide,
    All hushed their matin song !

But hark ! with advent of evening,
    The welkin rings again,
Again in the beautiful evening,
    They chant the morn's refrain !

I've sung my song in the morning,
    A brave, full-throated tune,
I've sung my song in the morning,
    And borne the toil of noon ;

But still, when cometh the evening,
    I want to sing once more,
Like birds in the beautiful evening,
    Hope's buoyant song of yore.

IN THE PRESENCE

(REV. xxii. 3-4)

THEY do His will, they see His Face, their foreheads
bear His name,
Who stand before the throne of God, and give the
Lamb acclaim ;
No curse can ever enter in, no night the glory dim,
Where shining souls, thus triple-crowned, eternal
praises hymn.

Obedience such as theirs, O Lord, teach me even
here below ;
The vision of Thy blessed Face in bright effulgence
show ;
Thy name and image, clear and pure, grave deeper
on my brow,
Till all shall see that I am Thine—my Lord and
Master Thou !

And thus shall curse, and night, and sin, like
shadows flee away
From out my life, and Light divine gleam through
it every day ;
The Throne of God and of the Lamb fixed deep
within shall be,
Heaven's life and bliss already mine, and through
eternity.

AU REVOIR

TO A PARTING GUEST

Now that you've found your way
   Here, to our country home,
Ne'er think, when seeking rest or change,
   In distant realms to roam.

Now that you've won your way
   Into our warmest hearts,
Ne'er think our love will lightly lend
   Your charms to other parts.

Now that you've brought us gain,
   By counting us your friends,
Your visits will, like summer suns,
   For dark days make amends.

Now that we've found each other,
   The richer are the springs
Of life's transcendent, purest joy,—
   The joy true Friendship brings.

TRANSFORMATION

Oh weary, dreary day,
Dark, dismal, dripping, grey;
I would some cheering ray
    Might pierce thy gloom;
If thou much longer stay,
    Thou'lt work my doom!

My brain conceives in vain
What pleasure thou canst gain,
To see the golden grain
    In soaking sheaves
Stand weeping in the rain
    No gleam relieves!

Yon reddening chestnut tree,
Drooping in misery,
Impatient waits to see
    The tarrying sun,
To flash but once in glee,
    Ere day is done!

Late rose, that fain would shine,
With radiance divine—

I see it droop and pine
  In bleak despair ;
Its grief, as if 'twere mine,
  I feel and share.

.   .   .   .

But hark ! the rustling trees
Bespeak the approaching breeze ;
Oh joy ! my spirit sees
  The greyness break ;
And look—the sun's release
  Bids all awake !

Come harvest, chestnut, rose,
With me your mirth disclose,
Let's sing away our woes
  In sunny praise ;
The world good promise shows
  Of brighter days.

MAKING AMENDS

TO A ROBIN

WHERE wast thou, singer late and lone, when all
    the woods were song,
When other birds their carols sang, through all the
    summer long ?
And now, when all their golden throats are hushed,
    I hear thy trill
This calm September morning, at my very window
    sill !

Methinks thy lay, sweet warbler, hath contrition in
    its tune,
As if sad memory charged thee with unfaithfulness
    in June
To take thy place among its choirs—and hence this
    late amends,
To win thy way, ere winter comes, to hearts and
    homes of friends.

And I, unfaithful steward too, will not attempt to
    blame ;
For smiling weather in our lives finds men, alas, the
    same !

The sunny present blinds the heart to scenes that
    gleam afar—
The Eternal Habitations where life's truest pleasures
    are.

And, only when our wayward hearts from God have
    ceased to roam,
Do wiser days our spirits urge to seek th' Enduring
    Home.
And so thy note, sweet penitent, hath taught me
    truths profound—
Thou art my boon companion ; thou my sympathy
    hast found !

"A DESERT PLACE"

A LONELY spot—with the hills around,
Bracken and heather profuse o'er the ground !
And through the dark trees away down by the
    shore,
A glimpse of our good ship—its week's work o'er—
Riding at anchor, majestic, tall,
The peace of the Sabbath day brooding o'er all !

A little churchyard—with tombstones grey
Buried in grass grown rank to decay :
Loved names graven—but moss o'ergrown
Veiling them quite, save from those alone
Who stoop to decipher with vision of love
The epitaphs quaint of the dear ones above !

An old grey church, simple, primitive, square,
Sheltered 'mid foliage lavish and rare :
Walls which no features artistic adorn,
Though within them "this one and that one was
    born " :
Modest its windows, yet through them, I ween,
True visions of heaven by pure hearts seen !

48

The sound of a bell from a belfry low !
And the scanty worshippers, solemn and slow,
Who have stood in the graveyard awaiting the hour,
Into the church to its music pour—
A company humble, even Christ's " two or three,"
God's glory and power, as aforetime, to see !

Psalms curious and old, sung to stately old strains,
Evan, Jackson's, St Lawrence—such old-time
    names !
While sitting we sing, and standing we pray,
Customs devout of a bygone day,
And never a worshipper slovenly seems,
'Tis a Bethel to all, with Jacob-dreams !

The preacher, turned sixty : voice soft and refined :
Earnest his manner and cultured his mind,
" Lay not up treasures on earth," his high theme,
Eternal things urging us all to esteem ;
And, by reasoning sound, to the truth we are driven,
That they are the wise who have " treasure in
    heaven."

How strange is it all : unspeakable ! vast !
That God, the Jehovah of Israel's past,
Is worshipped to-day in this corner remote—
Everywhere found where still lovingly sought !
That Palestine's Jesus is all the world's Christ,
Through growing dominion increasingly prized l

'Tis all of inscrutable Wisdom and Love,
Love that's around us as well as above ;
Wisdom which all through the ages has planned
That the Truth shall be published to every land !
Hence this Sabbath repose, this relief from each load,
In the worship of Nature and Beauty and God.

SUN AND CLOUD

When the sun's on the lea,
When the leaf's on the tree,
When but gladness I see,
    Be Thou near !
Thy great love on me shine ;
Thy rich beauty be mine ;
Thou my Bread and my Wine,
    Jesu dear !

When the cloud's in the sky,
When the leaves, driven, fly,
When but gloom I descry,
    Be Thou near !
Show Thy cloud silver-lined ;
Let Thy peace still my mind ;
All in Thee let me find,
    Jesu dear !

FAR HORIZONS

I LOVE the far horizons, the hills, the sky, the sea,
The gladsome light that lies o'er all, the breadth,
    the mystery ;
The petty ills that press me round—aye, and the
    great ones too,
Grow smaller far when seen against the spacious,
    open view.

My sorrow found me in the dark ; night's curtains
    closed me in ;
I could not see beyond my grief, I could no solace
    win ;
And all the weary vigils through, my burden grew
    amain,
Till night turned into morning, and I found the day
    again.

And then, when forth my window I beheld the
    world once more—
The distant hills, the stretching fields, the wide
    heavens bending o'er—
My soul expanded at the sight, strange strength my
    spirit found,
Care disappeared in holy calm, ineffably profound.

Even so, 'tis sure that grief and pain, and every
    earthly load
Their terror lose, and merge in good, when seen
    with vision broad :
God's wide and deep eternities show Time's worst
    trials small,
His boundless love and wisdom are the refuge from
    them all.

So I'll seek the far horizons still, the hills, the sky,
    the sea,
The gladsome light that lies o'er all, the breadth,
    the mystery,
And when at last, not far, but near, God's glory I
    shall see,
Earth's ills shall change to perfect bliss to all
    eternity.

THE MEASUREMENT OF LIFE

I WOULD not count my years in seasons,—
    Summer, Winter, Autumn, Spring,—
As if the changing skies were reasons
    For the joy or grief they bring.

I've seen dark Winters lit with Summer,
    Summers oft have Winter's cold ;
The vocal Springtide oft is dumber
    Far, of song, than Autumn's gold.

There's sorrow that may spell out gladness,
    Gladness that may work out doom ;
Life is not wholly joy or sadness,
    Unmixed light, or unmixed gloom.

So, give me rather that within me,
    While the swift years come and go,
Which spite of seasons still can win me
    Joy sublime in weal and woe,—

A buoyant trust that Love unceasing
    Guides me while I work and pray ;
A calm contentment, still increasing ;
    Hope, that shines from day to day.

THE INTERPRETING LIGHT

AHEAD, as my car with lightning speed,
Dashed on, nor gave e'en a moment's heed
To the darkling night, where the road rose high,
A wood on the crest engaged my eye.

Athwart the far sky's fast-thick'ning pall
It loomed in the dusk, a long black wall,
To the sight no charm did its flat length bring ;
It stood out a shapeless, loveless thing.

But round a sharp turn, as on we flew,
A quick transformation burst to view ;
There beyond the wood, as now west we hie,
Gleamed glorious and bright the sunset sky !

And 'gainst the great glare of that far heaven,
A meaning new to the scene was given,
Now the *wood* was *trees*, and to branch and leaf
The light streaming through gave bold relief.

That wood was our life, both first and last,—
Without far lights a conundrum vast !
But *with God behind*, to the reverent soul
A beauteous and transfigured whole !

WILD PANSIES

LIKE sapphires they glance at my feet,
I see their blue sheen on the hill ;
In yonder green hollow, on each grassy knoll,
They gleam in their beauty, entrancing my soul,
Where the lake and the woodland meet
The air with their fragrance they fill.

I know not what led me up here,
Afar from the beaten highway ;
But these radiant flowerets had scented the breeze,
Enamelled in vain with this blue of the seas
This upland remote—and none near !
Had I not chanced hither to stray.

I gaze, and rejoice, and adore,
At such loveliness blooming unseen,
For it tells the great truth that the beauty of God,
In lives He has touched, as in flowers of the sod,
Must oft its rich splendour outpour,
Where few to admire it have been.

In many a deep, quiet hollow,
On many a far distant field,

The flowers of His love in His children must blow,
Heaven's savour and light shedding forth as they
    glow,
  But their praise, now unsung, will sure follow,
  When they stand before God revealed.

NIGHTFALL

THE hot day is past, and I see no more
The moving crowd along the shore,
Men and women, and children gay,
Bent on their brief, bright holiday ;
Heaven's wide dome, and the deep, vast sea,
Telling their tale of eternity.

But now it is night, and I see below
Dim, shadowy shapes pass to and fro ;
Hushed is each voice, each earthly sound,
And the one thing left as I look around,
That light in the sky, that gleam on the sea—
Sure pledge of a new day's dawn to me.

When life's fleeting day draweth near its close,
When gathering night my spirit knows,
When faces familiar and voices dear
Grow dim and faint to my eye and ear,
God grant me the light of His face to see—
The dawn of His immortality.

REST

I sit in the calm of the Sabbath,
  At my window that looks to the hills,
Oh ! the landscape is fair—not a sound in the air,
  Save the music that silence distils.

Deep, deep is this stillness of Nature ;
  Sweet, sweet is this calm of the breast ;
Peace without, peace within — no discord, no
    din :
  Is this not God's pledge of His rest ?

Did ever the sun shine so golden,—
  E'en though it be Spring's early sun ?—
Did e'er his last rays lend so purple a haze
  To the hills, ere the daylight is done ?

The river—how placid, how slow,
  As it flows to its home in the main !
And the wood—passing fair, though its trees are
    still bare !
  Yet their leaves will soon flourish again.

The crocuses under my window,
  How bright in the newly-turned mould !

While the insects dance round them, entranced to
    have found them,
  Their joy and delight are untold.

Oh, why may this peace not endure ?
  Why this Sabbath die out with the sun ?
Why again, with to-morrow, life's labour and
    sorrow,
  While striving our journey to run ?

Be still, nor complain, O my heart !
  Thy peace in this hour is God-given,
To-morrow to brighten, its labour to lighten,
  A glimpse of the glories of heaven—

Of heaven, whose *sun* is Jehovah ;
  Whose *river*, the Water of Life ;
The *leaves* of whose *trees* bring glad healing and ease
  For sin, and for sorrow, and strife,—

An Eden, whose *flowers* never wither,
  Its life an eternal Spring,
Unbroken its charm by decay or by storm,
  Where loud praise through the ages shall ring.

FAITH AND SIGHT

I LOVE to see my children trustful
  Of the best things from my hand ;
Never doubting me, nor curious
  All to know and understand.

For trust is nobler far than knowledge.
  Faith than sight, a hundredfold ;
One the coward shows, the other
  Both for good and ill makes bold.

And so 'tis sure the Heavenly Father,
  Who His children's welfare plans
With a changeless love, and wisdom
  More consummate far than man's,

Rejoices most in those who trust Him,
  Leaning simply on His love,
These His best things here discover,
  And will win the best above.

LATE LABURNUM

Laburnum ! art thou mad, or bold,
In late October, grey and cold,
To hang out shining blooms of gold
    To wondering view,
When other trees are sere and old,
    And flowers are few ?

Thy kindred long have passed away ;
The lilac sweet, the hawthorn spray,
The gean, the rhododendron gay—
    All are no more ;
And thou alone dost greet the day
    With look of yore !

Hast thou awaked from sleep too soon,
Mistaking Winter's call for June ?
Or dost thou wish to grant a boon,
    Ere Autumn's dead,
To one who mourns the Summer noon
    Too swiftly sped ?

I cannot tell,—but this I know,
When I behold thee still aglow,

Still flashing forth fresh blossoms so,
    I'm taught the while,
To wait the coming frost and snow
    With thy bright smile !

THE GOLDEN RESIDUUM

Oh, where is the Summer I sighed for so long,
My sweet, golden Summer, all blossom and song ?
    Gone, all gone !

Oh, where is the glory, the glamour, the glee,
The radiant suns, the cool shade of the tree ?
    Gone, all gone !

Oh, where are the swallows, the bees in the flowers,
The games on the lawn, and the mirth in the bowers?
    Gone, all gone !

And where, all the friends whom the Summer
    brought here,
The faces, the voices, the fellowship dear ?
    Gone, all gone !

Oh, must I say " Gone " ? Must I harbour the
    thought,
And let my heart break ? Oh, the Summer is *not*
    Gone, all gone :

Its Spirit lives on ; for though seasons may roll,
The Summer's still here, nor can die from my soul—
    Love's not gone !

BROKEN LIGHT

THE splendours of the Summer sunset-glow
    Shot blood-red through the intercepting trees :
    And, fretful that my vision could not seize
Unblurred, the hues beyond, or fully know
The gorgeous scene that was obstructed so,
    In haste my discontentment to appease
    I climbed my tower, when lo ! I missed the trees !
Too dazzling was the sight ! The charm did go !

I must not seek all things to understand :
    If 'mid the tangled mystery of my days,
And cares that mar delights on every hand,
    I catch but gleams of glory through the maze,
I'll wait till in the All-revealing Land
    The full effulgence meets my tutored gaze !

THE GATE OF LIFE

IN MEMORIAM: A. M. C.

SAY they no trace of death is found
 At Springtide of the year ?
That only throbbing life around,
 Meets raptured eye and ear ?

Then, what is this I hear to-day—
 " He passed away at morn " ?
From 'midst the merry month of May
 Passed hence, as day was born !

Good friend of many happy years !
 A few brief weeks agone
He wandered here, all void of fears,
 Hopes never brighter shone !

We sang the charms of buoyant Spring,
 Its palpitating joys,
The music of its woods, that ring
 With song that never cloys.

My new rose-garden he appraised,
    Forecast its glory soon ;
Told how my rhododendrons blazed
    Around the lake last June !

And all the summer lay before,
    The glad earth to adorn . . .
Alas ! alas ! ah, nevermore !
    " He passed away at morn ! "

" At morn ! " Ah, well, the comfort's there l
    For never morning breaks
But grows to day, and passing *there*,
    His soul to noon awakes !

For death is but the gate of life ;
    And when our race is run,
We wake, to find beyond the strife
    Eternal Summer won !

A VAIN WISH

I WOULD the year would stay at the Spring,
   When all is young and gay,—
Would stay its pulsing life at the Spring,
   For ever, and a day !

The bursting bud is dearer to me
   Than full-blown leaf or flower,
Primrose and cowslip decking the lea,
   Than Summer's grandest dower.

The curlew's cry and the blackbird's song
   My soul more deeply move,
Than hum of bees the heather among,
   When suns oppressive prove.

There's no decay in merry Spring-time,
   No thought that brings despair ;
But bounding, buoyant life at the prime,
   And promise everywhere.

So, would the year but stay at the Spring,
   When all is young and gay,
With lightsome heart I'd cheerily sing
   For ever, and a day !

HOPE

THE hailstorm and sunshine contended,
  As I sheltered beneath the broad tree ;
Each its claim to be master defended,
  With furious persistency ;
    And so fierce was the challenge,
    So even the balance,
I could not the issue foresee.

But soon the stern fight was decided,
  When a bow threw its span o'er the storm,
And the cold blinding tempest subsided,
  While joy to my bosom leapt warm ;
    For that bow in the sky,
    Flashed its message on high,
" Let Hope all thy doubtings disarm."

Thus darkness and light through the ages,
  Wrath and mercy, alternate have reigned ;
Nor had all the world's mightiest sages,
  The key to the riddle attained ;
    Till the shining God-Man,
    On the clouds wrote Heaven's plan,
" Perfection through suffering gained."

And so, when mixed hope and despair,
  Make me waver at times to and fro,
To look upwards in faith I still dare,
  Though skies the more threatening grow ;
    For God's bow seen above,
    In the Son of His love,
With light keeps my spirit aglow.

A BROOK BY THE WAY

By the avenue, on to the mansion,
   There runs a clear stream all the way,
Pursuing my path, I can see it,
   And list to its roundelay ;
     Still gleaming and glancing,
     Still laughing and dancing,
   It carols along all day.

In summer its rippling music,
   Delight and refreshing instils,
In winter, by torrent-notes swollen,
   Its song all the dreariness fills ;
     Still leaping and bounding,
     Its echoes resounding,
   With rapture my soul it thrills.

And precious my " Brook by the way " is,
   As Homewards I journey along,
New life in His depths I discover,
   New courage I take from His song ;
     In gloom and in gladness,
     In sunshine and sadness,
   He is my Salvation strong !

THE HIDDEN GOD

I'D rather take my sorrow home,
   And hug it to my breast,
Than plunge it in the giddy whirl
   Of Pleasure's wild unrest.

Oh fools !   To think the trouble déad,
   To deem as drowned the pain,
Then see it from the mocking pool
   Come leaping up again !

Ah no !   I'll house it as a guest
   Who some great boon prepares ;
All inly clad in dazzling light
   Beneath the grey it wears.

And if I only humour it,
   I'll never rue the day
I took it in ; nor fretting flung
   The hidden God away !

FAREWELL

THE year is dying, dying,
    In lingering beauty dying !
The blush is fading from its face,
I see the shadows fall apace ;
    The golden year is dying !

The year is dying, dying !
    The withered leaves are flying
In clouds of amber through the air,
And in the branches gaunt and bare
    The chilly winds are sighing !

The year is dying, dying,
    With whispered farewells dying !
And man is mortal as the years ;
He buds, and blooms, then 'mid our tears
    'Neath fallen leaves is lying !

EASTER HYMN

Jesus lives !   To-day He's risen !
  Burst the fetters !   Void the tomb !
Jesus lives !   The Christ is risen !
  Vanquished death, the grave, the gloom !
      Hallelujah !
  Sealed is now their final doom !

Roman watch He all surprises,
  Rolls away with might the stone ;
Shroud and napkin leaves—and rises,
  Death's dominion to disown !
      Hallelujah !
  Man's dread enemy to dethrone !

Jesus lives !   The birds declare it ;
  Loud they chant their Easter song ;
Joyous chorus !   And they bear it
  All the woods and groves among !
      Hallelujah !
  Hark the merry vocal throng !

Jesus lives !   The firstling flowers
All take up the sweet refrain !
Earth, through all her waking bowers,
Bursting into green again ;
Hallelujah !
Blossoms opening to the strain !

Jesus lives !   The song comes stealing
To the ear, this holy day,
From the church bells, loudly pealing,
Calling us from Earth away ;
Hallelujah !
In His House our praise to pay !

This the truth of Easter morning,—
Jesus lives !   Omnipotent !
Lives !   Our languid souls transforming,
By His Presence immanent ;
Hallelujah !
In His resurrection sent l

Sing aloud, then, join the chorus,
Swell it to the courts above ;
Echo it to regions glorious,
Wafted on the wings of love.
Hallelujah !
Blend it with the choirs above.

Jesus lives!   To-day He's risen!
    Burst the fetters!   Void the tomb!
Jesus lives!   The Christ is risen!
    Vanquished death, the grave, the gloom!
       Hallelujah!
Sealed is now their final doom!

FLOOD-TIDE

I LOVE to see the cleansing tide
   Come rolling in amain,
Each blot and blemish of the shore
   Expurgating again.

I love to see the brimming tide
   Its flowing fullness bring,
Each empty creek and pining pool
   Anew replenishing.

I love the music of the tide,—
   Its voices manifold
That soothe and heal the heart of care
   With melodies untold. `

Oh Love, that cleanseth every stain,
   That every void can fill,
Whose deep, eternal harmonies
   Are balm for every ill,

Thy tide into my being pour,
   Flood me to overflow,
Till with Thy fullness satisfied
   Thy peace unplumbed I know !

CPSIA information can be obtained
at www.ICGtesting.com
Printed in the USA
BVHW090134211118
533638BV00012B/794/P

9 781331 780977